A LITTLE JAMIE BOOK

What It's Like to Be...
Qué se siente al ser...

MARTA VIEIRA

BY/POR REBECCA THATCHER MURCIA

TRANSLATED BY/
TRADUCIDO POR
EIDA DE LA VEGA

Mitchell Lane
PUBLISHERS

P.O. Box 196
Hockessin, Delaware 19707
Visit us on the web: www.mitchelllane.com
Comments? email us:
mitchelllane@mitchelllane.com

Mitchell Lane
PUBLISHERS

Printing   1   2   3   4   5   6   7   8   9

A LITTLE JAMIE BOOK

What It's Like to Be . . .   Qué se siente al ser . . .

What It's Like to Be . . .	Qué se siente al ser . . .
America Ferrera	América Ferrera
The Jonas Brothers	Los Hermanos Jonas
Marta Vieira	Marta Vieira
Miley Cyrus	Miley Cyrus
President Barack Obama	El presidente Barack Obama
Ryan Howard	Ryan Howard
Shakira	Shakira
Sonia Sotomayor	Sonia Sotomayor

Library of Congress Cataloging-in-Publication Data
Murcia, Rebecca Thatcher, 1962–
  What it's like to be Marta Vieira / by Rebecca Thatcher Murcia; translated by Eida de la Vega = Qué se siente al ser Marta Vieira / por Rebecca Thatcher Murcia; traducido por Eida de la Vega.
      p. cm. — (A little Jamie book = un libro "little Jamie". What it's like to be = Qúe se siente al ser.)
  Includes bibliographical references and index.
  ISBN 978-1-58415-852-3 (library bound)
  1. Vieira, Marta, 1986– —Juvenile literature. 2. Women soccer players—Brazil—Biography—Juvenile literature. I. Title. II. Title: Qué se siente al ser Marta Vieira.
  GV942.7.V515M87 2011
  796.334092—dc22
  [B]
                                                                    2010006526

ABOUT THE AUTHOR: Rebecca Thatcher Murcia graduated from the University of Massachusetts at Amherst in 1986 and worked as a newspaper journalist in Massachusetts and Texas for 14 years. Thatcher Murcia, her two sons, and their dog live in Akron, Pennsylvania. They spent the 2007–2008 school year in La Mesa, a small town in the Colombian department of Cundinamarca. She is the author of many books for Mitchell Lane Publishers, including *Meet Our New Student from Colombia, Ronaldinho, What It's Like to Be Shakira*, and *Dolores Huerta*.

DATOS BIOGRÁFICOS DE LA AUTORA: Rebecca Thatcher Murcia se graduó de la Universidad de Massachusetts en Amherst en 1986, y trabajó como periodista en Massachusetts y Texas durante 14 años. Thatcher Murcia vive con sus dos hijos y su perro en Akron, Pensilvania. Ellos pasaron el año escolar 2007–2008 en La Mesa, un pueblo de Colombia que está localizado en el departamento de Cundinamarca. Muchos de sus libros, como *Meet Our New Student from Colombia, Ronaldinho, Qué se siente al ser Shakira* y *Dolores Huerta*, han sido publicados por Mitchell Lane Publishers.

ABOUT THE TRANSLATOR: Eida de la Vega was born in Havana, Cuba, and now lives in New Jersey with her mother, her husband, and her two children. Eida has worked at Lectorum/Scholastic, and as editor of the magazine *Selecciones del Reader's Digest*.

ACERCA DE LA TRADUCTORA: Eida de la Vega nació en La Habana, Cuba, y ahora vive en Nueva Jersey con su madre, su esposo y sus dos hijos. Ha trabajado en Lectorum/Scholastic y, como editora, en la revista *Selecciones del Reader's Digest*.

PUBLISHER'S NOTE: The following story has been thoroughly researched, and to the best of our knowledge represents a true story. While every possible effort has been made to ensure accuracy, the publisher will not assume liability for damages caused by inaccuracies in the data and makes no warranty on the accuracy of the information contained herein. This story has not been authorized or endorsed by Marta Vieira da Silva.

PLB

What It's Like to Be... /
Qué se siente al ser...

MARTA
VIEIRA

Marta Vieira da Silva is one of the best professional soccer players in the world. She plays for the Los Angeles Sol in California. She is also the star of the Brazilian Women's National Team.

Marta Vieira da Silva es una de las mejores jugadoras de fútbol profesional del mundo. Juega para el Sol de Los Ángeles, en California. También es la estrella de la selección femenina de fútbol de Brasil.

Marta practices for hours every day. She has always played soccer. While she was growing up in Dois Riachos, Brazil, she did not have a coach or a team.

Marta practica durante horas todos los días. Siempre ha jugado fútbol. De niña, cuando vivía en Dois Riachos, en Brasil, no tenía entrenador ni equipo.

She learned to play soccer by playing against boys in her neighborhood. When she was ten, she joined the boys' team at her school. When she was fourteen, she took a three-day bus ride to Rio de Janeiro to try out for a professional team, Vasco da Gama. She was chosen for that team, and later went to Umeå IK in Sweden. To be able to run and kick the ball safely, Marta stretches before each game.

Aprendió a jugar fútbol enfrentándose a los niños del barrio. Cuando tenía diez años, se unió al equipo masculino de fútbol de la escuela. Con catorce años, hizo un viaje de tres días en autobús hasta Río de Janeiro para hacer las pruebas para entrar al equipo profesional Vasco da Gama. La escogieron y después se fue al equipo Umeå IK de Suecia. Marta hace estiramientos antes de los juegos para poder correr y patear el balón bien.

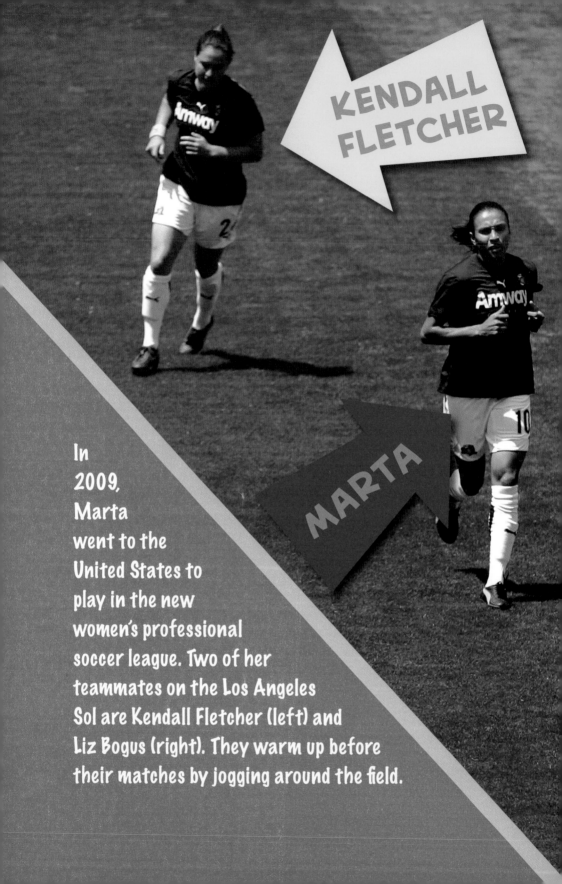

KENDALL
FLETCHER

MARTA

In 2009, Marta went to the United States to play in the new women's professional soccer league. Two of her teammates on the Los Angeles Sol are Kendall Fletcher (left) and Liz Bogus (right). They warm up before their matches by jogging around the field.

En 2009, Marta se fue a los Estados Unidos para jugar en la nueva liga de fútbol femenino. Dos de sus compañeras de equipo del Sol de Los Ángeles son Kendall Fletcher (izquierda) y Liz Bogus (derecha). Antes de los partidos, hacen ejercicios de calentamiento corriendo por el campo.

LIZ BOGUS

MANYA MAKOSKI

Kobe Bryant, a professional basketball star, is one of Marta's many fans. He loves to watch Marta's skill with a soccer ball. When he practiced with the Los Angeles Sol, he played in the goal.

Kobe Bryant, una estrella del baloncesto profesional, es uno de los muchos admiradores de Marta. Le encanta contemplar la destreza de Marta con el balón de fútbol. Cuando practica con Marta y el Sol de Los Ángeles, Kobe juega en la portería.

Marta grew up speaking Portuguese in Brazil. She learned Swedish while playing in Sweden. Now she speaks to her teammates in English. They talk about strategies between plays.

MARTA: 5'4"

Marta hablaba portugués en Brasil. Aprendió sueco mientras jugaba en Suecia. Ahora les habla en inglés a sus compañeras de equipo. Entre una jugada y otra, hablan sobre las estrategias a seguir.

BRITTANY BOCK: 5'7"

Marta throws the ball back into play from the sideline. The program lists her as a forward or striker, but she plays wherever she is needed to help her team win.

Marta lanza el balón al terreno desde la línea de banda. En el programa aparece como delantera o puntera, pero ella juega donde su equipo la necesite para poder ganar.

17

She will leap into the air to win a ball, and sometimes amazes everyone when she juggles or dribbles a ball around a defender. Her teammates congratulate her when she scores a goal.

Da saltos en el aire para hacerse con la pelota, y a veces, asombra a todos cuando gambetea y hurta el balón a un defensa del equipo contrario. Sus compañeras de equipo la felicitan cuando anota.

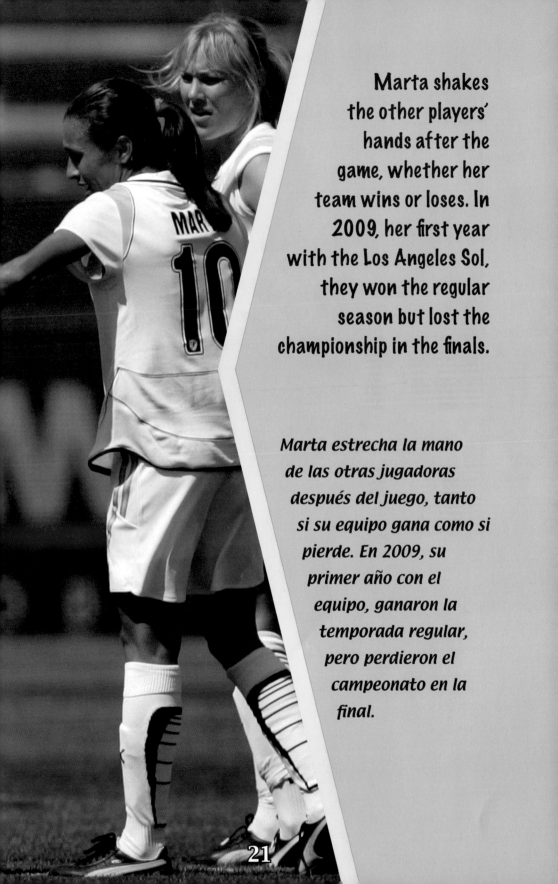

Marta shakes the other players' hands after the game, whether her team wins or loses. In 2009, her first year with the Los Angeles Sol, they won the regular season but lost the championship in the finals.

Marta estrecha la mano de las otras jugadoras después del juego, tanto si su equipo gana como si pierde. En 2009, su primer año con el equipo, ganaron la temporada regular, pero perdieron el campeonato en la final.

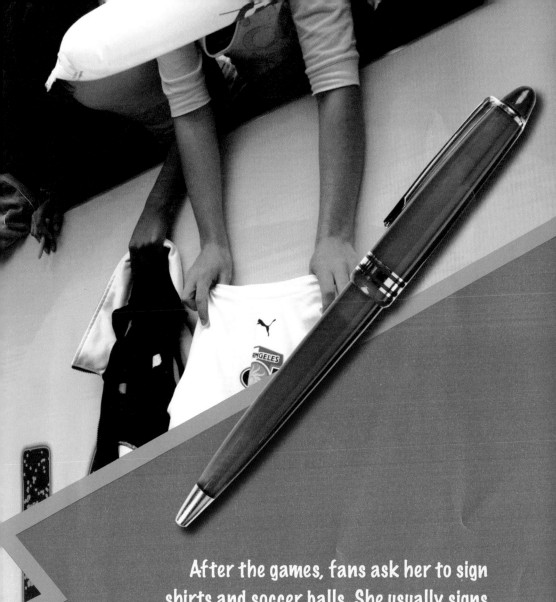

After the games, fans ask her to sign
shirts and soccer balls. She usually signs
her first name and her number, 10.

*Después de los juegos, los admiradores le piden que les firme
camisetas y balones de fútbol. Ella acostumbra poner su
nombre y luego su número, el 10.*

Kleiton Lima (left) is the head coach of Brazil's national soccer team. He and Marta often speak to the press before matches.

Marta first played for the Brazilian Women's National Team in 2007. In that game, the semifinals of the Women's World Cup, Brazil defeated the United States 4 to 0. Marta is famous for the way she scored one of the goals in that game. She flicked the ball in the air to get by one defender, and then turned the ball so quickly that another U.S. defender fell down trying to stop her.

Kleiton Lima (izquierda) es el director de la selección nacional de fútbol de Brasil. Él y Marta casi siempre hablan con la prensa antes de los partidos.

Marta jugó por primera vez en la selección nacional de fútbol femenino de Brasil en 2007. En ese juego, las semifinales de la Copa Mundial Femenina, Brasil derrotó a Estados Unidos 4 a 0. Marta es famosa por el modo en que anotó uno de los goles de ese juego. Levantó el balón por encima de una defensa, y luego hizo girar el balón tan rápido que otra defensa se cayó mientras trataba de detenerla.

Marta was named FIFA World Player of the Year in 2006, 2007, 2008, and 2009. She is the first soccer player ever to win the award four years in a row.

Marta se ha ganado el premio Jugadora Mundial de la FIFA en los años 2006, 2007, 2008 y 2009. Es el primer jugador de fútbol en haber ganado esa distinción cuatro años seguidos.

Anytime Marta plays, whether in Brazil, the United States, or international competitions such as the Olympics or the World Cup, the crowd goes wild when she gets the ball. They love to see her speed, and they love to see her score.

Siempre que Marta juega, ya sea en Brasil, en Estados Unidos o en competencias como las Olimpiadas o la Copa Mundial, el público enloquece cuando ella se apodera del balón. Les encanta su velocidad y verla anotar goles.

After her match, reporters interview her. They ask her about the awards she's won and how she scores so many goals. They also ask her something that everyone wants to know:

"What's it like to be Marta?"

Después del partido, los reporteros la entrevistan. Le preguntan sobre los premios que ha ganado y cómo puede anotar tantos goles. También le preguntan algo que todos quieren saber:

"¿Qué se siente al ser Marta?".

FURTHER READING/LECTURAS RECOMENDADA

Works Consulted/Obras consultadas

Canales, Andrea. "Women's Soccer Set to Try Again." *Sports Illustrated*, December 15, 2008.

FIFA.com. "Kleiton Lima's 2011 Dream." July 15, 2009. http://www.fifa.com/aboutfifa/developing/women/news/newsid=1081263.html

Jones, Graham L. "Kobe Bryant Welcomes Marta to Town." *Los Angeles Times*, March 6, 2009.

Sokolove, Michael. "Kicking Off." *New York Times Magazine*, April 1, 2009.

Turnbull, John. "Sweden, Northern Latitudes Helped Make Marta a Player of Sol Importance," *Global Game*, January 12, 2009. http://www.theglobalgame.com/blog/2009/01/sweden-northern-latitudes-helped-make-marta-a-player-of-sol-importance/

On the Internet

The Los Angeles Sol http://www.womensprosoccer.com/la

Marta's Official Web Site http://www.marta10.com/en/

En Internet

FIFA.com: Estadísticas FIFA de Marta http://es.fifa.com/worldfootball/statisticsandrecords/players/player=190358/index.html

Santos Futebol Clube: Futebol Feminino [Portuguese] http://santos.globo.com/feminino.php

INDEX/ÍNDICE

COVER DESIGN: Joe Rasemas. PHOTO CREDITS: Cover (top), pp. 8, 10, 12, 14, 18, 28—Victor Decolongon/Getty Images; cover (bottom), p. 22—Thorsten Wagner/Bongarts/Getty Images; pp. 3, 24—AP Photo/Hector Mata; p. 4—Silvia Izquierdo; p. 6—Jack Mikrut/AFP/Getty Images; p. 16—Ronald Martinez/Getty Images; p. 17—Teh Eng Koon/AFP/Getty Images; p. 20—Robert Laberge/Getty Images; pp. 27, 30—AP Photo/Keystone/Steffen Schmidt. Every effort has been made to locate all copyright holders of materials used in this book. Any errors or omissions will be corrected in future editions of the book.